A *Muslim's* Pocket Guide To Christianity

A *Muslim's* Pocket Guide To Christianity

Malcolm Steer

CHRISTIAN
FOCUS

Scripture quotations are from The Holy Bible, English Standard Version, copyright © 2001 by Crossway Bibles, a division of Good News Publishers. Used by permission. All rights reserved

Copyright © Malcolm Steer 2005

ISBN 978-1-84550-107-5

10 9 8 7 6 5 4 3 2 1

Published in 2005
Reprinted 2006 and 2009
by
Christian Focus Publications,
Geanies House, Fearn,
Ross-shire, IV20 1TW Scotland

www.christianfocus.com

Cover design by Alister MacInnes
Printed by Norhaven A/S, Denmark

CONTENTS

INTRODUCTION

I have been asked many times by Muslim friends concerning Christian beliefs. 'What do you Christians believe?' 'What are the main differences between Islam and Christianity?' And in view of the commonly held belief that Islam already contains Christianity, because Jesus is accepted as a great prophet of Islam, the question often arises as to why Christians have not progressed and become Muslims? Even more surprising for many Muslims is the question why anyone who is from a Muslim background would even consider 'going backwards' and become a Christian?

The purpose of this short book is to answer these questions, and many others, and to seek to clarify what is Christian belief in the same way that there are many books that help Christians to understand Islam.

In this age of tolerance, I believe it is important to respect one another's beliefs without causing unnecessary offence and yet at the same time not to compromise our beliefs or gloss over the differences.

I have taken part in a number of university debates with Muslim groups and each time my aim has been to discuss in a friendly atmosphere, clarifying both the common ground and the differences; and to do this in such a way that at the end of the debate I can sit down in the cafeteria with the other speaker and have a cup of tea with him! This is my purpose with this book and I hope that it will be read with this in mind.

I am well aware that many will not agree with all that is written here but I hope that the reader will at least accept it as an objective account of what the Christian position is and read it in that light.

ONE

ONE GOD, ONE WAY

What is Christianity about? Before considering specific Christian beliefs and practices it seems appropriate to ask the question 'What is the big picture?' If you are looking at a large painting, it is possible to look at it close-up and analyse it in detail but it is also good to stand back and get a view of the whole or to use an English expression: 'to see the forest from the trees'.

Jews, Christians and Muslims, unlike Hindus and Eastern Thought religions (who believe that history is cyclic and an ever-repeating circle), believe that history is a straight line with a beginning and an end.

Where does Christianity fit into this line? Many mistakenly think that Christians have uprooted Jesus (Isa Al Masih) from history and become followers of a person who lived 2,000 years ago but who has no connection with history either before he came or afterwards! However, this is not the case. Everything fits together and there is a unity about God's plan and purpose.

Christians believe that God created human beings in order to have a relationship with them and in the beginning, during the time of Adam and Eve, this was the case. However, man and woman were not created like robots but given a free-will, and being deceived by Satan disobeyed God's command and as a result lost that spiritual relationship with God. Spiritual and physical death entered the world leading to separation from God and eventually eternal death.

The situation continued to deteriorate to such an extent that God destroyed all through the flood and recommenced with Noah and his family. Sin continued to rule though as seen in the incident of the Tower of Babel (Genesis 11). In the light of these great universal events such as the Fall of humankind, the Flood and the scattering of people around the world after the building of the Tower of Babel (Genesis 3–11), God puts into effect his plan of restoration in order to bring blessing and salvation to all humankind.

Abraham and the People of God

Abraham is chosen (Genesis 12) and through his family, which grew into the nation of Israel, a foundation was laid that would prepare the world for the coming blessing and salvation. God entered into a special covenant relationship with his people and through Moses (*Musa*) and Joshua led the people out of the captivity of Egypt, through the wilderness and into the Promised Land.

All of this is recorded in the Bible (*Kitab al-moqaddas*) and in the part known as the Old Testament*, certain principles are found which help show that there is not only one God but also only one Way to him. For example, through the history of the People of Israel the following principles are evident:

1. People are sinful and have been separated from God and are under condemnation deserving to be punished for their sins.
2. There is nothing that human beings can do, e.g. good works, by which they can merit God's acceptance.
3. However, God in his mercy has provided the principle of sacrifice so that a 'sinless' animal can take the place of the sinful person and this leads to forgiveness.
4. God gave the Law through Moses so that his people might know how to live as the people of God.

God raised up priests who represented the people and who carried out the sacrifices on the altar of

---

* The Old Testament books in the Bible (*Kitab al-moqaddas*) are the Jewish Scriptures comprising of the *'Torah'* or the *'Tawrat'* i.e. the five books of Moses as well as the *'Zabur'* i.e. the Psalms of David, and altogether 39 books including the books of the Prophets. In common usage *'Tawrat'* is often used to refer to the whole of the Old Testament.

the tabernacle (a temporary structure established in the wilderness) or in the temple built later on by Solomon. God also raised up prophets, who represented Him and who brought God's Word to his people. After great leaders like Moses and Joshua, other leaders known as Judges and then kings were raised up in order to lead the people of God.

However, despite all this, there was the desire for something better and complete. There seemed to be constant failure on the part of the people and even with some of its leaders, all prompting the need for change. Therefore in the Old Testament there are many references to a coming figure that became known as The Messiah (*Al Masih*, The Anointed One or The Christ). Moses spoke of a coming special Prophet; there was the expectancy of a perfect High Priest who would live for ever and in the light of the failure of the kings, the promise from God of a perfect King who would reign for ever.

There were great limitations and restrictions under this old covenant, mainly because of the need for animal sacrifices, the need for a special place in which to carry out the sacrifices and also, in view of the constant failings and shortcomings, the need for the people to be changed themselves. So in the Old Testament, there is mention of a coming new covenant, which among other blessings included a perfect sacrifice for sin, a new temple/meeting place and the pouring out of God's Spirit on all believers involving a change of the human heart. It is for this

reason that the Bible is divided into two sections:
the Old Testament (*'Ahd al-Qadim*) and the New
Testament (*'Ahd al-Jadid*) for the word 'testament'
means 'covenant'.

Therefore to summarise the expectancy of the
Old Testament, the people were longing for:

- A perfect Prophet, High Priest and King.
- A perfect sacrifice for sins.
- A new covenant.
- A new temple.
- An inner transformation of all believers by
  God's Spirit.

The Coming of the Messiah

From the end of the Old Testament until the birth
of Christ there is a gap of 400 years and 'silence'
from God. But God knew what he was doing and as
the Apostle Paul said, 'When the fullness of time
had come' God sent Christ to this world.

As I was reminded by my College Professor
of 'The History of World Civilisation' when I was
studying in Tehran many years ago, the most appropriate time, from a political, cultural, social and
security point of view, for the Saviour of the World
to come was the time when he came. This was the
best time in history that would ensure and help the
expansion of the message of Christ.

Prophet

Why did he come? Does he just fit into the long line of prophets who came before and brought God's message or is there something else happening here?

In one sense he is a prophet and he certainly fulfils the prophecy of Moses regarding 'The Prophet' who was to come. In fact, people at the time of Jesus recognised this and said, 'This is indeed the Prophet who is to come into the world' (John 6:14 & 7:40*) and later on the Apostle Peter confirmed this when he was preaching in Jerusalem (Acts 3:22). On at least two occasions Jesus also used the title (Mark 6:4, Luke 13:33).

But in what sense is he a prophet?

Christians believe that although it is true that he was born of the virgin Mary yet this was not the beginning of his existence. To put it simply, Christ has always been around. He is the Word of God (*Kalamatollah*). As the *Injil* says, 'In the beginning was the Word, and the Word was with God and the Word was God. He was in the beginning with God...And the Word became flesh and dwelt among us...' (John 1:1-2,14).

---

* These references are taken from the New Testament (*Injil*) in the Bible. Strictly speaking '*Injil*' refers to the first four books known as 'The Gospels', but in common usage '*Injil*' refers to the whole of the New Testament.

What makes Jesus unique is not only that he prophesies about the future as other prophets do, or that he brings messages from God, again as other prophets do, but that God is speaking to us through his whole being and personality. Jesus is the image of the invisible God (Colossians 1:15) and the God who in the past spoke through the prophets is in these last days speaking to us through the person of Christ (Hebrews 1:1-2). Through his life, teaching, miracles and his presence on earth Christ is showing us what God is like and that there is a God who loves and cares for us. What Christ does is the action of God himself and therefore as God's representative he brings a complete and full revelation of the living God.

High Priest and Sacrifice

However, this is not enough: to be a prophet is only part of the reason why he came, the main reason lies elsewhere. The history and teaching of the Old Testament clearly demonstrate that sin has separated us from God and that the most important human need is forgiveness of our sins. Therefore Christ not only represents God but, like the High Priests of old and as a true human being, he represents us. However the amazing truth is that in representing us he not only does that through his life but also in his willingness to become both priest *and* sacrifice. By his death he takes our place and becomes the perfect sacrifice for our sins. Jesus himself said that he had not come to be served but to serve and give his life as a ransom for many (Mark 10:45).

Therefore the message of Christianity is that Christ through his life and death both reveals God to us and reconciles us to God. His resurrection confirms these truths, for it is through the risen living Christ that we now have access to God.

For this reason, the word 'Saviour' has a particular meaning for Christians. In a debate that I was involved in – one of those debates where afterwards I enjoyed a cup of tea with the Muslim speaker – the speaker stated that the human problem was one of ignorance and therefore our need was to hear from the prophets concerning God's will. My response was to agree with him on this point but to add that our problem is not just one of ignorance but one of inability.

There is much law and teaching in the Old Testament, but because of the effects of sin and the weakness of us human beings, we lack the power to change and obey God's law. Someone who is drowning and who cannot swim does not need someone to come and start teaching the person how to swim. Their primary need is for a lifesaver who can dive in and rescue them. For this reason our primary need is not teaching – that follows later – but salvation, and when we study the Gospel records at the time of Christ's birth, we observe that the messages from the angels to the shepherds and Mary's future husband, Joseph, is of a Saviour being born; one who is known as the Saviour of the World (John 4:42). John the Baptist, a contemporary of Jesus and a great prophet said about Jesus: 'Behold, the Lamb of God who takes away the sin of the world!' (John1:29)

If Christ was only a prophet and had only come to bring teaching, then he would simply fall in line with all the other prophets. But not only has God in these last days spoken through Christ but '... he has appeared once for all at the end of the ages to put away sin by the sacrifice of himself' (Hebrews 9:26).

King

This matter of forgiveness of sins is also connected to the theme of Jesus being the Son of David (*Dawud*) and fulfilling the dream of a future king who would reign forever. For this reason when the angel appeared to Mary concerning the birth of Jesus he confirmed that he would be given the throne of his father David and that of his kingdom there would be no end (Luke 1:32-33).

At the time when Jesus lived, the Jews were being oppressed by the Romans and there was a great expectancy that when the Messiah appeared he would deliver them from this oppression and establish a new independent political reign.

Some of the followers of Jesus were thinking along this line and therefore became very disillusioned when instead of this happening, Jesus was taken and killed. This sense of despair is clearly evident in an incident recorded at the end of Luke's Gospel.

On the day that Christ rose from the dead, two of his followers were returning home from Jerusalem to their village called Emmaus. Jesus drew near to them, but in the words of Luke 'their eyes were kept from recognising him'. When asked why they were sad, one replies and among other comments says, 'we had hoped that he was the one to redeem Israel'. In response, Jesus replies 'O foolish ones, and slow of heart to believe all that the prophets have spoken! Was it not necessary that the Christ should suffer these things and enter into his glory?' And beginning with Moses and all the Prophets, he interpreted to them in all the Scriptures the things concerning himself. (Luke 24:26-27)

Later on their eyes were opened and they recognised him. Jesus then appears to his disciples and clearly gives the reason why he had to die. 'These are my words that I spoke to you while I was still with you, that everything in the Law of Moses and the Prophets and the Psalms must be fulfilled.' Then he opened their minds to understand the Scriptures, and said to them, 'Thus it is written, that the Christ should suffer and on the third day rise from the dead, and that repentance and forgiveness of sins should be proclaimed in his name to all nations, beginning from Jerusalem.' (Luke 24:44-47)

I have often purposely misread this verse in public by inserting 'people of Israel' rather than 'all nations' in order to emphasise the point that Jesus did not just come for that time only or just for the Jews. The living Christ is for all and for all time and he meets the most important need of the human heart i.e. forgiveness of sins.

If only people at that time had realised that, contrary to their thinking, Jesus was indeed thinking of oppression but not political, social or economic oppression. Political and religious systems come and go but even the best systems in the world can only change the outward. They are not radical enough. The root cause of oppression is sin in the human heart and the question is who can change human beings? In the first place, people need to be forgiven of their sins, restored in their relationship with God and experience inner transformation by God's Spirit.

Christ is king but his kingship is of a different type to that found in the world. This is illustrated in one of the well-known miracles in the New Testament (John 6). Jesus provided food for at least 5,000 people from only five loaves and two fish, but when the people wanted by force to make him king, he withdrew, and went alone to a nearby mountain.

Furthermore, when later on he was asked by Pilate, the Roman governor, about his kingship he replied 'My kingdom is not of this world. If my kingdom were of this world, my servants would have been fighting that I might not be delivered to the Jews. But my kingdom is not from the world' (John 18:36). Christ's is a spiritual kingdom where by his Holy Spirit he wants to enter our lives so that our relationship can be restored with God. With Christ ruling in our hearts, God can begin to fulfil the very purpose for which he created us.

For this reason, Christ spoke about sending his Spirit after he returned to heaven. Following the resurrection, Christ spent 40 days with his disciples and then ascended. Ten days later, the Holy Spirit was poured out on the disciples and, with the power and presence of Christ in their lives, they commenced their mission of spreading the good news around the world.

The death and resurrection of Christ from the dead brought into effect the new covenant and the internal work of God's Spirit ensured that the original blessing of salvation made to Abraham many years ago was now accessible to all. The sacrifice of Christ meant an end to all the animal sacrifices and the end of the need for a special building with all its ceremonies. In fact as people began to respond to the message and became believers so they were joined together into a new community which itself was like a spiritual temple.

In conclusion to this chapter, let me make two points:

Firstly, in order to emphasise the point that Christianity in essence is not just based on the teaching of Christ, we observe that it is based rather on certain specific historical events such as:

- The coming of the eternal Word of God into time and space as a human being.
- His death providing a perfect sacrifice for sin.
- His resurrection from the dead three days later.
- His ascension back to heaven 40 days later and
- The coming of the Spirit of Jesus, i.e. the Holy Spirit on all believers on the Day of Pentecost ten days later.

The combination of these events constitutes the essence of the Christian message.

Secondly, to return to the title of this chapter, the one and true God, who has been at work in history, has shown through the story of the descendants of Abraham, as recorded in the Old Testament, that there is only one way to him. All the previous rev elations were a preparation for the coming of the Christ, the Saviour of the world, who would remove the barrier of sin for all time and for all peoples by a perfect sacrifice.

TWO

BELIEFS AND PRACTICES
OF CHRISTIANS

1) BELIEFS

- <u>GOD</u>. Jews, Christians and Muslims all emphasise the Unity and Oneness of God, and also his majesty, transcendence and sovereignty. God is all-powerful, all-knowing and present everywhere. He is the creator God who not only created everything but also sustains everything.

  However the Bible not only emphasises these attributes of power but also his moral attributes such as his love, mercy, grace, holiness, justice and righteousness. God is love and it is the relationship between his holiness and love that becomes an important issue in Christian belief.

  Furthermore, the Bible teaches that this love is expressed within the Unity and Oneness of God through the three persons of the Trinity: Father, Son and the Holy Spirit (see chapter 3).

- <u>THE HOLY BOOKS AND PROPHETS</u>. God has revealed himself in history and these historical events and the meaning of these events and other messages from him are recorded in the holy books known as the Bible (*Kitab al-moqaddas*). The first part known as the Old Testament (*Tawrat*) records creation and God's dealings with his people of that day. The names of many prophets are found as well as their writings. They were God's representatives, so to speak, who spoke to the people on behalf of God.

  The second part known as the New Testament (*Injil*), and containing 27 books, records the coming of the Messiah (*Al Masih* or The Christ) and details of his life, death and resurrection, the beginning and expansion of the Church and letters to the new Churches written by the Apostles leading to a final book mainly about future events. The first four books of the New Testament relating to the life of Christ are known as the Gospels (see chapter 5).

  It is important to point out that although there are many different writers and that the 66 books in the Bible were written over a period of about 1,500 years, yet the Holy Spirit so guided each writer that what is written is the Word of God. These books provide a basis for all Christian belief.

- HUMANITY. Again, Jews, Christians and Muslims are agreed that God is the source of everything and that he created humanity. For this reason we as human beings are not here by chance but have value and significance. Human beings were created without sin and there was perfect communion between God and humankind.

  However, God created human beings with a free will, with the ability to choose their own destiny. For this reason, Christians do not hold to a fatalistic view of God or believe that everything, both good and evil, has been predetermined. Therefore one of the most significant events in history was the time when Adam and Eve disobeyed God and were thrown out of the Garden of Eden. It is significant because it was the fall of humanity that brought about a radical change in humankind's relationship to God, with others and in himself. Sin entered and brought about the fall of the whole of humanity and that from then on, all human beings would be born with a sinful nature.

- SIN. For this reason, from a Christian point of view, sin is not simply seen as a series of actions that break rules of prohibition, but it is a state of sinfulness that exists in each human being. In other words, the issue is not just *sins* but the nature of *sin* that has affected all aspects of human nature including thoughts, motives and attitude. Humankind is cut off from God, is spiritually dead and needs life and forgiveness. 'For all have sinned and fall short of the glory of God' wrote the Apostle Paul (Romans 3:23). Because of his holiness and righteousness, God is grieved by sin and he expresses himself with a divine hatred of sin. Sin therefore not only breaks a law but also fellowship between the Creator and his created beings. 'Behold, the Lord's hand is not shortened, that it cannot save; or his ears dull, that it cannot hear; but your iniquities have made a separation between you and your God, and your sins have hidden his face from you so that he does not hear' (Isaiah 59:1-2).

• <u>SALVATION</u>. What can be done to rescue the situation? One matter is clear and it is that there is nothing that humankind can do. Not only does the Bible teach that human beings are sinful, dead and cut off from God, but it also shows that people by themselves cannot change the situation. That is why it is the Christian conviction that good works, including religious acts do not bring us to God. In fact the Bible states that in God's sight, because of his absolute righteousness even our 'good works' are like dirty clothes (Isaiah 64:6). If humankind is dead, then whatever a person does cannot produce life. God and only God can help.

But how can God help? It is true that he is a God of mercy but the difficulty is that he is also a God of justice. The question is how can God forgive sinful people who are already under the condemnation of death and at the same time maintain his holiness, righteousness and justice?

The story is told of a judge whose son committed a crime and who was brought before him for the sentence. Perhaps onlookers thought that the judge would be favourably lenient as it was his son before him, but in a court of law justice has to be done. To everyone's amazement the judge fined his son the maximum amount permitted. It was clear that he did not have the money to pay and that he would have to go to prison. Following the court proceedings the judge left, took off his formal court robes and as a father went and showed mercy to his son by paying the fine.

Although this is a defective illustration of God's dealings with humankind, the principle is the same. In view of his holiness, justice and righteousness he cannot overlook sin or simply forgive it. Justice needs to be done and humanity is under condemnation deserving the punishment of death. 'For the wages of sin is death' (Romans 6:23). But God out of his love, mercy and grace provides a way by which he can show mercy and satisfy his justice and wrath against sin. He provides a substitute to take the place of the condemned sinner. But who is this substitute?

This is where Christ enters the picture. Christ who was from the beginning and who was without sin not only enters the world with a divine nature as God's representative, but he comes as a human being with a human nature in order to represent us. By his death he takes our place and dies the death that we deserved to die. 'For Christ also suffered once for sins, the righteous for the unrighteous, that he might bring us to God' (1 Peter 3:18).

Therefore on the basis of Christ's death, forgiveness is available to all who turn from their sin and accept God's offer of forgiveness in Christ. God raised Christ from the dead and he is alive for evermore. Therefore this forgiveness and acceptance is available now to all who believe in Christ as their own personal Saviour.

• DAY OF JUDGEMENT. We are living at a time when there is an opportunity to respond to God's invitation to receive forgiveness but this time of opportunity will come to an end. Christians believe that on a day fixed by God, Christ will come again and the end events will commence.

One of these events is the Day of Judgment. Those who have been forgiven will be in the presence of God but for others there is a judgment – a judgment that is based on how they have lived and their punishment will be on this basis. This can be clarified by stating the following. When God looks at our world he does not see us according to our ethnic or religious backgrounds. In reality there are only two groups in this world – those who have been forgiven and those who are still in sin and remain under condemnation. 'God is not wishing that any should perish but that all should reach repentance'. However the next verse begins 'But the day of the Lord will come like a thief…' (2 Peter 3:9-10).

2) PRACTICES

Christians believe that when a person accepts God's offer of forgiveness of sins they are born again and become a new creation. God's Spirit gives life to the person who was spiritually dead and a new life begins.

Christianity is not full of do's and don'ts because one of the blessings of the new covenant is that God writes his law on the Christian's heart and guides by his Holy Spirit. Furthermore, the motivation in living a life that pleases God is no longer to earn forgiveness or acceptance but rather as an expression of thanks for God's acceptance and forgiveness.

There is therefore an expectation that new believers will grow and become mature believers and that their Christian life will be built on the following four pillars:

- PRAYER. Now that the relationship has been restored with God it is natural to be in contact with the one who is also referred to as 'Father in heaven'. Christians are referred to as his sons and daughters and in fact the whole essence of the Christian life is tied up with the relationship that they now have with the Living God. For this reason there are no set rules on how, when or where to pray but in their own language they can speak to him both when alone or with others. Prayer consists of different aspects and includes praise and worship to God for who he is and for what he has done, confession of sins, thanksgiving for his daily blessings and bringing requests for their own needs and the needs of others.

    Similarly with fasting, there are no rules, but many Christians have private times when they fast, usually for a specific purpose and abstain from food for a period of time. Some Christians use the 40 day period before Easter (known as Lent) to abstain from various things and spend time in meditation and preparation for the remembrance of Christ's death.

- THE BIBLE. If through prayer Christians talk to God, then through reading and meditating on the Bible, they allow God to speak to them. For this reason it says 'All Scripture is breathed out by God and profitable for teaching, reproof, for correction, and training in righteousness, that the man of God may be competent, equipped for every good work' (2 Timothy 3:16-17). Therefore most Christians make time each day to read a part of the Bible. It is spiritual food and is as important as ordinary food. However, it is not read just for the sake of being read but in order to challenge and lead to obedience.

- THE CHURCH. The Church is God's new society. Christians do not believe that it is possible to 'Christianise' society in a way that some other religions seek to direct and order all aspects of human affairs and life. The Christian view is different. Firstly, free will has to be respected and secondly change cannot be imposed on society or carried out by force. However, those who have experienced the new life in Christ become members of an alternative society that continues to operate within the existing society. Firstly, such people automatically become members of the world-wide Church and then secondly, become members of a local Church where they live. So primarily the Church is not a building but is made up of believers meeting together.

In this new community, all become brothers and sisters and benefit from fellowship and interaction with each other. This normally takes place on a Sunday (the day Jesus rose from the dead) but there are other activities during the week. As the Church constitutes a spiritual temple, worship and praise through singing spiritual songs and prayer is an important element of the life of the Church. There are also opportunities to receive teaching from the Bible and so preaching is another important element.

New Christians are baptised as a testimony to others that they have become followers of Christ and as an act of remembrance for Christ's death, there is a simple ceremony consisting of bread and a cup of grape-juice known as 'breaking of bread' or 'Holy Communion' which takes place either weekly or periodically. Giving is also important and on a regular basis members give a proportion of their income to God. These collections take place at each local Church.

- WITNESS. Every Christian is expected to share their faith with others and pass on the good news (meaning of the word 'Injil'). So even though the bad news is that our spiritual situation is desperate, similar to someone awaiting execution, yet God in his love and mercy has reached out to us in order to save us and restore the relationship with himself. Therefore all Christians want others to know about this good news. Furthermore, one of the last commands of Christ, known as the 'Great Commission', was that Christians are to go to the whole world and tell people about this message (Matthew 28:18-20). Witnessing can be done individually or by inviting seekers to special meetings where the message of Christ is explained.

THREE

MISUNDERSTANDINGS ABOUT CHRISTIANITY

We all know what it is like to be misunderstood. Although we might use the same words and expressions, they convey different meanings to different people. Some might even reject the use of certain words and expressions because their understanding of what they mean is not only different to Christians but also contrary to their own belief system.

This is particularly true of the way that certain Christian concepts have been misunderstood. Over the centuries certain misunderstandings have developed and we will consider five of them. They are:

1) that Christians believe in three gods and that the Trinity is made up of God, Mary and Jesus.
In response, it is important to clearly emphasise the oneness of God and state that the Trinity has nothing to do with the number of gods but with the nature of the one true God. It must also be emphasised that Mary is not God or part of God, but that

the Bible shows this one God revealing himself as Father, as Son and as Spirit or we can say that God reveals himself as Creator, Word and Spirit. This does not mean that God changed himself from one thing to another, for he has always existed in these three ways.

Of course, God is a mystery far above our thought and no one can explain exactly how God exists in three ways. In the same way it is difficult to explain the doctrine of the Unity of God which is defined in terms of the relation of God's eternal attributes to each other and to God's eternal essence. Is that not also a metaphysical puzzle? The doctrine of the Trinity is simply the way the Christian tries to summarise what the Bible teaches about God, Jesus and the Holy Spirit. Rightly understood, this doctrine exists to defend the unity of God.

2) that the expression 'Son of God' used of Christ refers to a merely carnal relationship in which God took a wife and produced a son.

This expression does not refer to the physical coming of Christ but to the eternal relationship that Jesus had with God who is called 'Father'. Mary was simply the human agent by which Jesus was introduced into the world. Furthermore, when expressions like 'son of something' are used in everyday speech they convey a spiritual meaning like a metaphor and do not imply physical sonship. Examples: 'son of the road', 'son of a leopard' 'sons of thunder'. The expression 'Son of God' is used only in a spiritual sense.

However, even when this is understood, the question is how can it be shown that Jesus eternally existed and was not a created being? A popular title for Jesus found in the Qur'an is the expression 'the word of God' (*Kalamatollah*) and if this is linked with Islamic belief concerning the nature of the Qur'an it helps to understand the pre-existence of Christ.

Both Christians and Muslims agree that God is eternal and that God's Word is eternal. The eternity of God and his Word are one and the same thing, for God is one. Moreover, both Muslims and Christians agree that God bridges the gulf between the infinite and finite by revealing this eternal Word to his finite creation. For Muslims, God expresses his eternal Word within the created world through the book called the Qur'an. Hence, most Muslims call the Qur'an the eternal Word of God. For Christians, God expresses his eternal Word within the created world through a person called Jesus. Hence, the Bible speaks about the eternal Word of God becoming a human being, the man Jesus.

This matter of God speaking to humanity through his Word can be illustrated by human speech. Where was my word before it came out of my mouth? In my brain and in my thoughts; but if you cut open my head can you find my word there? In some mysterious way my word and I are the same and cannot be separated. Whatever my word does, it is I who am doing it. How could Jesus have authority to forgive sins (Mark 2:1-12) or be judge on the Last Day (Matthew 25:31-33)? This is only possible because Jesus is the Word of God. What he does is the action of God himself.

So God's eternal Word came to have a human life among people as Jesus Christ. He is the image of the invisible God and as he himself said 'he who has seen me has seen the Father' (John 14:9) and when he was praying said 'And now, Father, glorify me in your own presence with the glory that I had with you before the world existed' (John 17:5).

3) that the death of Christ would have been an unworthy ending to his life and is not necessary to provide forgiveness of sins.

There are many that have genuine difficulties over the teaching of the death of Christ especially as an atonement for sins. Firstly, some reject it on historical grounds and argue that God would never have allowed such a great prophet to die in the way that Christians say he died. Secondly, and more importantly, many reject the concept of the need for someone to die as an atonement for sins. God does whatever he wills and so if God wants to forgive he simply forgives. God is merciful and in addition, good works such as prayer, fasting and almsgiving can help 'atone' for a person's sins.

In response, it must first of all be said that any fair reading of the New Testament (*Injil*) shows that the death and the resurrection of Christ are central to the New Testament message. Major portions of the Gospel accounts are dedicated to these events. Jesus himself continually predicts these events and in fact reprimands his disciples for failing to understand that as the Messiah he must suffer, die and rise from the dead. Jesus saw himself as the fulfilment of many Old Testament prophecies relating to his suffering and death. He determined to sacrifice himself out of love for humanity and in obedience to God. So that, although it is true that the people of his day opposed Jesus and plotted to kill him, yet Jesus in accordance with the will of God voluntarily laid down his life. God approved the sacrifice that Jesus made and vindicated his claims by raising him from the dead.

It is important to understand the meaning of Christ's death. Firstly, it puts an end to all other sacrifices. A study of the sacrifices of the Old Testament shows that the people approached God by way of sacrifice. The sacrifice of Jesus takes away our guilt and brings us into fellowship with God.

Secondly, Christ's death assures us of our forgiveness. However, this cleansing from sin is not automatic. It needs to be accepted by faith through trusting in the one who died for our sins. The way of salvation is not a matter of first trying to be righteous in order to make ourselves worthy of salvation, but rather first coming as an unworthy sinner and accepting God's free forgiveness as a gift.

Thirdly, Christ's death reveals the horror of sin and the righteousness of God. Sin deserves to be judged and punished. But God in his mercy allowed the suffering and judgment to be carried out by Jesus the Saviour. Through Christ crucified, God offers us forgiveness, but also shows us his righteousness.

4) that Christianity is a Western religion.

Many believe that as the followers of Christianity are mainly found in Western countries, called Christian countries, all the inhabitants are Christian and as these countries represent Christianity so their actions reveal what Christianity is really like.

In response it is important to be reminded of the origin of Christianity. Jesus Christ was born in Palestine and it is here that the origin of Christianity is to be found. Palestine is the land that joins the three great continents of Asia, Africa and Europe and it was from here, using the famous Roman roads and trade routes, that the Christian message was able to spread rapidly in all directions. In fact, for the first 400 years or more, the great centres of Christianity were to be found in Africa and Asia. Furthermore, in the 20th century, there has been phenomenal growth in some non-western countries such as China and South Korea.

It is also helpful to draw a comparison here with Islam, because as it is a total system having important national, social and political implications, it is easy to regard Christianity in the same way. However, the true essence of Christianity is spiritual and primarily concerns our relationship with God. Although the Christian message should affect us in a total way yet it is, by nature, very different from the concept of a total system.

Furthermore, it is important to point out that although Christianity is not individualistic yet it demands an individual response. As has been pointed out already, there is no way that we can 'Christianise' society. The Church as a community is an essential element of the Christian message but no one is naturally born into that community. Therefore a clear distinction needs to be made between nominal and committed belief.

5) that the Bible is not reliable, having been changed or corrupted from its original form.

The Qur'an frequently refers to the holy books of the Jews and Christians and calls such people the 'People of the Book' (*Ahl al-kitab*). Muslims view the Qur'an and Islam as a continuation and fulfilment of previous revelations and therefore regard all previous prophets and holy books as proclaiming essentially the same message as the Qur'an. However, differences do exist and many believe that the differences have been caused by changes and corruptions introduced by Christians and Jews into the Bible during the course of history. It is also asserted on the basis of the Qur'an, that the Scriptures previous to the Qur'an have been abrogated by the Qur'an.

However, in actual fact the Qur'an does not teach that the previous Scriptures given to Jews and Christians are textually unreliable or have been abrogated. The Qur'an supports the existence, availability, integrity and universal significance of these Scriptures. It encourages all to believe these Scriptures and even confirms them (Sura 5:43-52, 70-72). In fact, if Muhammad himself is in doubt, the Qur'an tells him to appeal to Jews and Christians and to their Scriptures (Sura 10:95).

A multitude of ancient manuscripts of the Bible in its original languages and in translations abundantly testify to the preservation and integrity of the biblical text. Even if a group of unbelievers had wanted later on to make changes to the Bible, it would have been an impossible task in view of the number of copies of Greek and Hebrew Scriptures available and the way that these had been scattered throughout the world. Total suppression of these Greek and Hebrew Scriptures would have been impossible.

There is a question elsewhere in the book concerning the Gospels (see chapter 5) but suffice it to say here that there is abundant evidence to show that it is perfectly reasonable to accept the four Gospel records as historically reliable and authentic.

Often the impression is given that there were hundreds of other accounts of the life of Christ that were systematically destroyed after the Council of Nicea. (See chapter 4 concerning the 'Gospel of Barnabas'.) But it must be pointed out that no single Council was responsible for arbitrarily collecting and proclaiming a list of books as canonical. Rather, the New Testament books became authoritative because the Church regarded them as divinely inspired with apostolic authority (whether direct or indirect). The first ecclesiastical councils to classify the canonical books did not impose something new upon the Christian community but rather codified what was already the general practice of those communities.

There is one other important point that needs to be mentioned in conclusion of this section and that concerns the purpose behind the Bible. The purpose of the Scriptures is to lead us to Christ. They are not an end in themselves but rather a means to an end. There is no salvation in the Scriptures themselves; neither do we 'worship' them. Jesus said to the Jews: 'You search the Scriptures, because you think that in them you have eternal life; and it is they that bear witness about *me*, yet you refuse to come to me that you may have life' (John 5:39-40).

FOUR

STUMBLING BLOCKS

Some have gone further than simply having misunderstandings about the Christian message and
have brought some arguments against the message
of Christ. So therefore it seems only fair that in a
book designed to help give a better understanding of the Christian message these arguments are
briefly examined. It is said, 1) that the Gospel of
Barnabas is the only authentic reliable Gospel,
2) that the Bible contains prophecies concerning a
future prophet after Christ, and 3) that the message
of Jesus was for the people of Israel only.

Let us look at these three points.

1)The Gospel of Barnabas: is it authentic?

Some claim that the Gospel of Barnabas is the only
known surviving Gospel written by a disciple of Jesus and that it was accepted as a canonical Gospel
up until the Council of Nicea in AD325. From that
time, it is argued, the Christian Church has ignored
and suppressed it. It was supposed to have been
rediscovered by a Christian monk called Fra Marino

who came across an Italian manuscript in the Pope's private library in 1590. He smuggled it out of the library, read it and became a Muslim.

In fact, the only known existing text of the Gospel of Barnabas is in Italian in the Vienna Library. This text, dated in the sixteenth century, was edited and translated into English by Laura and Lonsdale Ragg and published in Italian and in English in 1907. Since then it has been translated into Arabic, Urdu and other languages. In the 1907 publication, the introduction gave internal and external evidence to show that the Gospel was a medieval forgery but this introduction has been omitted from most publications.

The Gospel of Barnabas incorporates a number of normal allegations: Jesus is not the Son of God; Judas Iscariot, not Jesus, dies on the cross; Jesus prophesies the coming of Muhammad, etc. It contains most of the events found in the four Gospels but with many things artfully turned to favour Islam.

Now if we refer to ancient manuscripts of the New Testament dating back to pre-Islamic times and to which the Qur'an refers and testifies to their truth, we find no record of a Gospel attributed to Barnabas. Neither is there any mention of it in the list of the books which constitute the Bible by the Church fathers. Furthermore, according to the New Testament, Barnabas was not one of the twelve disciples of Jesus and was not even

named Barnabas until after the ascension of Christ
(Acts 4:36). All external and internal evidence indicates that the Gospel of Barnabas is a forgery of
European origin, dating from about the fourteenth
century or later.

The author, a Christian who embraced Islam,
simply utilises materials from the biblical Gospel
accounts, omitting and altering at will to suit his
purposes. But apart from this and other geographi-
cal and historical errors, one example from this
work will indicate that he not only contradicts
the Gospel but also the Qur'an. In many places
'Barnabas' makes Jesus declare that he is not the
Messiah, but that Muhammad will be the Messiah.
This statement contradicts both the Gospel and the
Qur'an since in both Jesus alone is the Messiah.

Of course not all Muslims accept the Gospel
of Barnabas as a genuine Gospel account. In fact
one Muslim scholar has said, 'In the light of the
Christian rejection (of the Gospel of Barnabas as
a genuine gospel) the contention that this work is
genuine can be validated only when a copy of it
that antedates the mission of the Prophet has been
discovered and brought to light – which thus far
has not been possible' (quoted in 'The Gospel of
Barnabas: An Essay and Inquiry' by S. Abdul-
Ahad and WHT Gairdner. Henry Martyn Institute
of Islamic Studies, India, 1975).

2) Is a future prophet after Christ foretold in the Bible?

Many believe that the coming of Muhammad was foretold in the Bible and particularly appeal to two sections to substantiate this claim i.e. Deuteronomy 18:15,18 in the Old Testament (*Tawrat*) and the Gospel of John 14–16 in the New Testament (*Injil*).

With the first passage, the contention is that the prophet was to be raised up, not from the people of Israel but from among their brethren. It is argued that Ishmael, father of the Arabs, was a brother of Isaac and the phrase 'from among your brethren' clearly refers to the Arabs and to Muhammad as the Arab prophet.

In response, it is an undeniable fact that Jews are more truly brothers to each other than to Arabs, as history has shown. Furthermore, the word 'brethren' most naturally refers to the people of Israel (refer to Deuteronomy 17: 14,15; Leviticus 25:46). Even if we accept the correctness of the interpretation of 'brother' here, why should Ishmael be selected rather than some other close relative of Abraham or even of Isaac or Jacob, such as, for example, Jacob's brother Esau, from whom the people of Edom are descended?

Interpretation of this passage needs to pay heed to the biblical evidence which refers to its fulfilment. Jesus said, 'If you believed Moses, you would believe me, for he wrote of me' (John 5:46), inferring that the prophecy of Moses relates to Jesus himself as the prophet to come. Acts 3:17-26 and 7:37 clearly understand Jesus to be the fulfilment of the Deuteronomy verses.

In the passage from John's Gospel, it is claimed that the Greek word *paracletos* which is translated 'helper' should read *periklutos* or 'praised one', which would have the same meaning as Ahmad or Muhammad. However, no sound evidence in the New Testament manuscripts supports this assertion. Furthermore it is obvious from the context of these verses that the Helper can only refer to the Holy Spirit. This is not only clearly stated anyway in John 14:26 but verses 16-17 indicates that the Holy Spirit '... will be with you for ever... You know him, for he dwells with you and will be in you'. None of these passages from John's Gospel suggest that the disciples were to wait some five centuries before the fulfilment of his promise. In Acts 1:5 we read that the time of the Spirit's coming was very short. It was subsequently fulfilled just ten days after Jesus' ascension on the day of Pentecost.

3) Was Jesus a national prophet to Israel only?

It is understandable that many have difficulties over the universal claim of Christ that he is 'the way, the truth and the life. No one comes to the Father except through me' (John 14:6) or the words of the Apostle Peter 'there is salvation in no one else, for there is no other name under heaven given among men by which we must be saved' (Acts 4:12). One way to dispute these claims is to demote him and say that he is the last national prophet of Israel. He therefore loses all significance for the Gentiles. Statements such as 'I was sent only to the lost sheep of the house of Israel' (Matthew 15:24) and Matthew 10:5-6 are used to support this claim.

However, there are of course passages in the Bible that do speak of his universal ministry. For example, Jesus said, 'I am the light of the world' (John 8:12). There are passages in the Old Testament concerning the Servant of the Lord and his universal mission, passages which, according to the New Testament, find their fulfilment in Jesus (compare Isaiah 42:1 with Matthew 12:15-21). However, Christians gladly agree that Jesus, while on earth, to a large extent limited his ministry to the people of Israel. The reason for this goes back to Genesis 2:2-4 where we read that through the seed of Abraham all the nations of the earth will be blessed. So Jesus confesses to the Samaritan woman at the well (John 4) that 'Salvation is from the Jews' (note: not 'to the Jews').

Only the Jews could understand the significance of Christ, for he was embedded in the history and the inspired writings of Israel. The Jews were waiting for him. He had to be a Jew (Deuteronomy 18:15) and he had to be a descendent of Judah and the house of David (Genesis 49:10, 2 Samuel 7:13). Every Jew expected the Messiah, even though they did not recognise him at this coming.

So only the Jews – and only after they had understood him – could proclaim him to others; hence all the apostles were Jews. Jesus after his resurrection, clearly explained to his disciples that this message of 'repentance and forgiveness of sins should be proclaimed in his name to all nations, beginning from Jerusalem' (Luke 24:47). Therefore Jesus ordered his disciples to 'make disciples of all nations' (Matthew 28:19,20), and even though it took a while for the apostles to understand this, eventually they began to carry out this command.

An illustration might help our understanding. In many countries, without an irrigation system, the fields have no water. Therefore the water is channelled and localised by means of canals, aqueducts, tunnels and channels until it reaches the fields where it is then allowed to flow out freely. Now concerning the water of life we can say that the channels for the life-bringing water were the Jews and that the apostles were the final sluice gates which brought the water to the fields that represent the world.

It is therefore consistent that in his lifetime Christ prepared the channels that would bring the water to the fields. Even his help to the Gentiles, such as the Roman centurion, served as a lesson for his own disciples. He said, 'Truly, I tell you, with no one in Israel have I found such faith. I tell you, many will come from east and west and recline at table with Abraham, Isaac and Jacob in the kingdom of heaven, while the sons of the kingdom (Jews) will be thrown into the outer darkness…' (Matthew 8:10-12).

FIVE

FREQUENTLY ASKED QUESTIONS

1) Why are there four Gospels?

Many readers of the New Testament are surprised to find that there are four Gospels rather than one, and as these have been written by four men it appears that we do not even have the Gospel (*Injil*) of Jesus.

However, the truth is that we only do have one Gospel and in fact it is the Gospel of Jesus the Messiah. He himself is the Gospel. The word 'Gospel' means good news and this good news is found in the person of Christ. Therefore the four Gospel accounts in the Bible are four accounts of one and the same Gospel. Thus the account by Mark is really the Gospel of Jesus the Messiah according to Mark ('The beginning of the Gospel of Jesus Christ...' Mark 1:1). The fact that we have four records actually strengthens the argument of the accuracy of these records. If there was only one record, one might question how we know the record is a valid one, whereas, in fact, we have four records of the events.

If four people were to go to Trafalgar Square in London and sit in four corners and describe Nelson's Column and everything else that they see, their written testimony would be different. Their accounts would not contradict but rather compliment each other. It is true that there are differences in the Gospel accounts, but they are presenting a complete picture of the person of Christ. In each case their target audience is different and also their emphasis concerning the ministry and mission of Christ is different.

This can be illustrated, for example, by referring to the matter of the genealogies and the four Gospel writers: Matthew, Mark, Luke and John. It is commonly understood that Matthew, mainly written for Jews, wants to show that Christ is truly the Messiah. Therefore he includes a genealogy and shows clearly that Christ is the son of David and the son of Abraham. Mark, who in emphasising the servanthood of Christ does not even include details of his birth or a genealogy but commences with the ministry of Christ. Luke in showing that Christ was truly human does include a genealogy and not only goes back to David and Abraham but also to Adam. John, on the other hand, wants to show that Christ has existed from the beginning. So he does not include details of Christ's genealogy or his birth but goes back beyond David, Abraham and Adam to eternity and states that 'In the beginning was the Word' (John 1:1).

2) Why are there divisions in Christianity?

Christianity is mainly divided into three branches – Roman Catholic, Orthodox and Protestant. The first point to make is that if one were to draw a circle, this circle would include these three branches. In other words, these three branches are in agreement with the main fundamental truths of the Christian message including most, if not all, with what is written in this short book. There are other groups, such as the Jehovah Witnesses and the Mormons who would be outside this circle because they have different beliefs concerning the essential Christian truths.

There are many similarities between the Roman Catholic and Orthodox Churches who separated from each other in 1054 AD; Catholics becoming known as the Church in the West and the Orthodox as the Church in the East. Both put a strong emphasis on tradition and ceremony.

The main difference between these Churches and the Protestant Church is over the matter of authority. When Martin Luther protested about the state of the Church in his time where he in fact was one of its ministers, he believed that the Church had deviated from the principles of early Christianity. To put it simply, the Catholic Church in addition to the Bible, regards traditions and official statements of the Church and Pope as authoritative. So for example, the very existence of the Pope, the exaggerated beliefs concerning Mary and the need to confess sins to a Priest are all concepts not found in the Bible. In the famous words of Martin Luther our authority is ' Scripture alone, through faith alone and by God's grace alone'.

Therefore the Protestant movement was a protest reaction against this situation and wanted to return to the authoritative truths found alone in the Bible. Of course, the Protestant Movement itself is made up of many different Church groups, largely because of differing views over Church structure and organisation. However, in many countries there is an informal alliance that unites Bible believing Churches together and although there is great variety between these Churches on Church structure, method of worship and secondary doctrinal matters, there is broad agreement on Christian belief and practice.

3) What special days and festivals are there in Christianity?

In view of the strong emphasis on the spiritual aspects of Christian belief, many Christians, unlike many of the more traditional Churches, do not make a great issue about keeping special 'holy days' or ceremonies.

However, in view of the facts mentioned in the first chapter, that Christianity is founded on historical events rather than just teaching, these events are remembered in the Christian calendar. The two most important are Christmas when the birth of

Christ is celebrated and Easter comprising of 'Good Friday' and Easter Sunday when respectively the death and resurrection of Christ are remembered. Other significant days would be the Ascension, which always falls on a Thursday, forty days after Easter, and the Coming of the Holy Spirit ten days later on the Day of Pentecost and which always falls on a Sunday.

Christmas is always December 25th but the time of Easter which is based on the Jewish lunar year moves backwards and forwards each year and normally occurs during late March or in April. It is worth mentioning that New Year's day is not normally regarded as a Christian event even though it is connected with the Christian calendar.

SIX

FINDING THE PEARL OF GREAT VALUE

In this final chapter let us summarise what we have been considering by answering the question 'what is unique about Christianity?' What blessings can be found here that cannot be found anywhere clse? Or to use a picture that Jesus uses concerning a merchant in search of fine pearls, who, on finding a pearl of great value goes and sells all that he has and buys it (Matthew 13: 45-46). What is the pearl of great value in the Christian message?

There are least four issues that Christians would argue are special and unique:

1) Knowledge of God: the concept of revelation and how the one true God reveals himself through Christ.

People everywhere are sincerely seeking after God. However, an over-emphasis on the greatness and power of God can make him rather remote, impersonal and unknowable. Religion can become a tightly defined legalistic system rather than a relationship of love that exists between God as Creator and human beings as the created.

What is unique in Christianity is that the one true personal God who loves humanity and who desires a relationship with human beings has revealed himself in a personal way through Christ so that all might come to know him as their heavenly Father.

Therefore, there is no greater joy and privilege than knowing God and knowing him as father.

2) Forgiveness of Sins: the concept of atonement and how the one true God forgives us through Christ's sacrifice.

Most religions call on people to repent but such a call depends on the concept of sin, that is, on what one is called to repent from. Some believe they are sinners because of some evil which they have committed, and not because of 'original sin' (see sections on 'humanity' and 'sin' in chapter 2) or the nature of their hearts. Therefore, the call is to repent from infringements of the ritual and moral code and to seek to wipe out small sins by good deeds.

The biblical concept of sin shows that the forgiveness needed is more than the cancellation of bad debts in a great book of accounts. It is of the utmost importance to realise that all are rebels against God, because of their very thoughts, speech, work and life. Everyone, therefore, needs forgiveness in order that a right relationship between God and the individual can be established. Sin separates from God and it is only on the basis of Christ's sacrifice that true forgiveness can be experienced, and the individual be brought into fellowship with God. In actual fact many people are plagued by feelings of guilt over wrongs committed and are sincerely seeking for assurance of forgiveness.

Therefore, there is no greater joy and privilege than knowing that sins have been forgiven.

3) Assurance of salvation: distinguishing between law and grace as the basis of acceptance before God.

Many religions teach that God forgives sin, but the basis of forgiveness is different. In some, salvation rests upon one's own shoulders and obedience to the law, while in Christianity it rests purely and solely upon the grace of God. Others tell a person what they must do to earn salvation; Christianity tells a person what God has done to give them salvation. Therefore in the former there is no assurance of salvation, for in this world people cannot know for certain whether God has destined them for paradise or hell. However, in Christianity, even though they do not consider themselves to deserve God's forgiveness, yet on the basis of the death of Christ, God offers salvation to be received as a gift by faith. Good works are important in Christian living but salvation and acceptance by God is not dependent upon these works.

Therefore, there is no greater joy and privilege than knowing that God has accepted the individual.

4) Change of heart: distinguishing between outward reform and inward change.

In many countries a determined effort is under way by its religious leaders to bring their society more in line with the principles, laws and regulations of that religion. Sometimes such actions bring the religious hierarchy into conflict with certain sections of the population who react and rebel against such rules and regulations that seem to be negative and restrictive.

It is also illustrated by the teachings of Christ where we learn that what defiles human beings is the corrupt heart, which cannot be changed by mere outward reform. People are unable to make new characters for themselves. They cannot make an evil desire become good or change a love for sin into a love for righteousness. It is only new life and power from God that can change a person and give that person the capacity to live a life of righteousness in obedience to the will of God.

Therefore there is no greater joy and privilege than experiencing this new life and power through God's Holy Spirit.

May the Living God help each one to choose this 'Pearl of great value' whatever the cost might be.

APPENDIX

For those wishing to make a further study of the Christian Faith, correspondence courses in English and other languages are available from:

'Word of Life', PO Box 14, Oldham, OL1 3WW, UK
email: info@word.org.uk
Website: www.word.org.uk

For those wanting literature about the Christian Faith in English and other languages contact:

'Kitab', PO Box 315, Oldham, OL1 3YW, UK
email: kitab.uk@domini.org
Website: www.kitab.org.uk